THE STORY OF THE CLEVELAND CAVALIERS

THE NBA:
A HISTORY
OF HOOPS

THE STORY OF THE
CLEVELAND
CAVALIERS

NATE FRISCH

CREATIVE EDUCATION

Published by Creative Education
P.O. Box 227, Mankato, Minnesota 56002
Creative Education is an imprint of The Creative Company
www.thecreativecompany.us

Design and production by Blue Design
Art direction by Rita Marshall
Printed in the United States of America

Photographs by Basketballphoto.com (Steve Lipofsky),
Corbis (Bettmann), Getty Images (Nathaniel S. Butler/
NBAE, Jesse D. Garrabrant/NBAE, David Liam Kyle/
NBAE, David Liam Kyle/Sports Illustrated, Manny Millan/
Sports Illustrated, Joe Murphy/NBAE, Greg Nelson/Sports
Illustrated, Nivek Neslo, Dick Raphael/NBAE, Gregory
Shamus, Carl Skalak/Sports Illustrated), Newscom (DAVID
T. FOSTER III/MCT/ABACAUSA.COM, Mitchell Layton/
MCT, Albert Pena/Cal Sport Media, Z Sports Images/
ZUMAPRESS), USA TODAY Sports (David Butler II)

Library of Congress Cataloging-in-Publication Data
Frisch, Nate.
The story of the Cleveland Cavaliers / Nate Frisch.
p. cm. — (The NBA: a history of hoops)
Includes index.
Summary: An informative narration of the Cleveland
Cavaliers professional basketball team's history from its
1970 founding to today, spotlighting memorable players
and reliving dramatic events.
ISBN 978-1-60818-426-2
1. Cleveland Cavaliers (Basketball team)—History—Juvenile
literature. I. Title.

GV885.52.C57F75 2014
796.323'640977132—dc23   2013037445

CCSS: RI.5.1, 2, 3, 8; RH.6-8.4, 5, 7

First Edition
9 8 7 6 5 4 3 2 1

Cover: Guard Kyrie Irving
Page 2: Forward LeBron James
Pages 4–5: Guard Kyrie Irving
Page 6: Guard Delonte West

TABLE OF CONTENTS

COURTSIDE STORIES

INTRODUCING...

BLUE-COLLAR BEGINNINGS

CLEVELAND'S DOWNTOWN AREA SITS ON THE BANKS OF THE CUYAHOGA RIVER.

wampy, damp, inclement. Such unpleasant terms could be used to describe the southern shores of Lake Erie, but during the westward expansion of the United States, the area was too practical to pass up. Proximity to Lake Erie and the Ohio River system meant shipping and transportation opportunities, and in 1796, General Moses Cleaveland laid out plans for a city that would become a vital hub of distribution. That city—Cleveland, Ohio—became even more relevant with the development of railroads, and it was soon a web of canals and railways. Cleveland and its residents earned an ongoing reputation for their resourcefulness and hardiness.

Perhaps seeking a break from their blue-collar lifestyles, Clevelanders rallied behind a local professional baseball team (eventually called the Indians) starting in 1901 and football's Browns in 1946. In 1970, a new National

Basketball Association (NBA) franchise hoped to tap into that devoted fan base. Eager to get the locals involved right off the bat, the club asked prospective fans to submit ideas for the team's name. The chosen moniker was the Cleveland Cavaliers, referring to the mounted soldiers who had contributed to the expansion and settlement of much of the U.S. including Ohio.

Cleveland winters were cold, and the Cavaliers hoped a warm seat and an exciting basketball team would get residents flocking to Cleveland Arena. But while owners could turn up the heat in the stadium, the 1970–71 roster was a chillier matter. The first "Cavs" squad was made up of unproven rookies and castoffs from other NBA teams. Guiding the team would be head coach Bill Fitch. Even he had his doubts about the club's prospects. Commenting on the roster and its chances of success, he quipped,

DICK SNYDER

COURTSIDE STORIES

THE MIRACLE OF RICHFIELD

Twenty miles south of the city of Cleveland lies the suburb of Richfield, home of the Coliseum, where the Cavaliers played from 1974 until 1994. The 1975–76 season in the Coliseum is still known to some as the "Miracle of Richfield." In Cleveland's first-ever playoff series, it clashed with the favored Washington Bullets and their star forward, Elvin Hayes. After a narrow Game 1 defeat, Cleveland battled back in Game 2. The game culminated in forward Bingo Smith draining a long-range, game-winning shot with two seconds left. In Game 5, guard Jim Cleamons duplicated the feat, hitting another game-winning buzzer beater for the Cavs. The series concluded with Game 7 in Richfield, where guard Dick Snyder sank a clutch bank shot in the game's waning seconds, giving Cleveland an 87–85 win in front of 21,564 screaming fans. "The fans would get rolling a half hour before the game," said Cavaliers guard Austin Carr about the series. "They'd be stomping on the floor, 'Let's go, Cavs! Let's go, Cavs!' It was to the point where the entire building was shaking. It was unbelievable, and that's how it went every game."

BINGO SMITH

Bobby "Bingo" Smith was one of the original Cavaliers, playing on the 1970–71 expansion team. Although never a superstar, Smith offered dependability to the franchise. While the Cavs' roster seemed to be completely overhauled every few years, Smith was among the few mainstays throughout the '70s. The durable forward rarely missed a game and averaged 13.2 points a night during his Cleveland career. Smith also added identity to the team. He wore a big Afro most of his career—whether it was the popular style or not—and was known for his high-arcing rainbow jumpers. Although there wasn't a three-point line in the NBA until his final year in Cleveland, Smith loved launching long-range shots. "He's a streak shooter and gives you a big lift when he gets hot," said Cavs guard Walt Frazier. It was a 25-foot bomb by Smith in the final seconds of a 1976 postseason contest that clinched the first playoff win in Cavaliers history. The Cavaliers retired his jersey number (7) the same season he left the team and while he was still active in the NBA.

"Remember, my name is Fitch, not Houdini."

The Cavaliers lived up to the low expectations, losing 15 straight games—often in blowout fashion—to open the season. They finally eked out a 105–103 victory in a matchup against a fellow expansion team, the Portland Trail Blazers, only to lose another 12 games in a row. The Cavs improved marginally as the season went on but still finished with a miserable 15–67 record.

On the upside, a pair of promising young forwards, John Johnson and Bobby "Bingo" Smith, emerged as players the franchise could build around. Before its second season, Cleveland used its first-round pick in the NBA Draft to select All-American guard Austin Carr from the University of Notre Dame. The 6-foot-4 Carr immediately added much-needed scoring punch to the lineup, and it took the 1971–72 Cavaliers just 39 games to match their win total from the previous season.

Unfortunately, Carr was hampered by a foot injury, and the team spiraled down the stretch, winning just 8 of its last 43 games. After that season's end, the Cavaliers traded away one All-Star guard, Butch Beard, and received another, Lenny Wilkens, but the moves did little to boost the team up the standings the next two years.

Then, in 1974, Cleveland's fortunes seemed to start heading in the right direction. The club drafted 6-foot-8 forward Michael "Campy" Russell and traded for tough, 6-foot-11 forward Jim Chones and sharpshooting guard Dick Snyder. With Smith, Carr, Chones, Snyder, and Russell on the floor of the Cavaliers' new arena, Richfield Coliseum, Cleveland finally had enough talent to make a run at the NBA playoffs. Unfortunately, injuries to Carr and Chones left the 1974–75 Cavs at 40–42, one game short of a postseason berth.

WAYNE EMBRY

Wayne Embry was an accomplished NBA player. The 6-foot-8 forward/center played for three different teams from 1958 to 1969, earning five All-Star selections with the Cincinnati Royals and one NBA championship with the Boston Celtics. Still, his greatest mark on the NBA may have been in becoming the first African American general manager in league history when he took over that position for the Milwaukee Bucks in 1972. His first real success as a general manager, however, was in Cleveland. In Embry's inaugural season in Ohio, the team had perhaps the best off-season in franchise history, acquiring rookies Brad Daugherty, Mark Price, and Ron Harper. This laid a solid foundation for team success that would remain in place for nearly a decade. During Embry's 13 seasons as general manager, the Cavaliers earned 10 winning seasons and 9 playoff berths. Perhaps the worst thing that could be said about Embry was that his timing was bad, as the Cavaliers' peak years coincided almost exactly with the dominating dynasty of Michael Jordan and the Chicago Bulls.

15

GLIMMERS OF HOPE

GUARD CLARENCE "FOOTS" WALKER WAS THE FIRST CAVS PLAYER TO GET A TRIPLE-DOUBLE.

The ending to the Cavaliers' 1975–76 season was to become known as the "Miracle of Richfield," but the way the year began was hardly miraculous. Cleveland lost 11 of its first 17 games before making an early-season trade for All-Star center Nate Thurmond. While playing with the Golden State Warriors and Chicago Bulls, Thurmond had earned a reputation as one of the league's toughest defenders and rebounders. Although the veteran was past his prime, his forceful personality and presence in the low post were just what the young Cavaliers needed.

Mixing youth and veterans with talent at many positions, Cleveland gathered steam, winning 43 of its remaining 65 games and winning the Eastern Conference's Central Division to reach the postseason. Cleveland's first-ever playoff series went a full seven games, with the Cavaliers

BRAD DAUGHERTY

POSITION CENTER
HEIGHT 7 FEET
CAVALIERS SEASONS
1986–94

In many ways, Brad Daugherty's basketball career seemed to be in a hurry. Daugherty entered college at age 16. In the 1986 NBA Draft, he was snatched up by Cleveland with the first overall pick. He was an All-Star and led the Cavaliers to the playoffs in only his second season. In just eight seasons, Daugherty set the franchise's all-time career scoring and rebounding records. More important than his individual accomplishments, however, was his impact on the team's success. "This team's really built around Brad," said Cavs forward John "Hot Rod" Williams. "Mark [Price] controls it, but Brad is the focus." The Cavaliers reached the playoffs six times during Daugherty's eight years with Cleveland. Never the most athletic of players, Daugherty instead excelled through polished skills and a strong understanding of the game. He had a soft touch around the basket, including a nearly unblockable jump hook, and his stability made him a reliable anchor for the Cavaliers. Unfortunately, the career that had taken off quickly also came to a fast finish. A back injury ended Daugherty's playing days when he was just 28 years old.

nudging out the Washington Bullets by just two points in the pivotal Game 7. In fact, three of the Cavs' four wins came as the result of clutch baskets in the final seconds. Unfortunately, Chones, Cleveland's leading scorer, suffered a broken foot during practice before the next series, and the Cavaliers lost their second-round matchup with the Boston Celtics in six games.

The Cavaliers marched to the playoffs the next two seasons but were eliminated in the first round each time. By 1979, Thurmond had been retired for two years, and veterans such as Smith, Carr, and Chones were beginning to slow down. Cleveland had acquired future Hall of Fame point guard Walt Frazier in 1977, but he, too, arrived near the end of his career. After Cleveland limped to a 30–52 mark and missed the playoffs in 1978–79, Fitch stepped down as head coach.

After improving to 37–45 in 1979–80, Cleveland lost more than 50 games in each of the following 4 seasons. At the very lowest point, the 1981–82 Cavaliers duplicated the miserable record from their inaugural campaign 11 years earlier, going 15–67.

Still, there were highlights. Forward Mike Mitchell used an accurate shooting touch and great leaping ability to average 19.3 points a game during 4 seasons in Cleveland. After Mitchell left the Cavs in 1982, eccentric shooting guard World B. Free took over as the top scorer. Free specialized in long-range bombing and rarely passed on an opportunity to fire away. "World sincerely believes every shot he takes will go in," said Cavaliers guard John Bagley. "A lot of times, he's right."

In 1983, local businessman Gordon Gund purchased the Cavaliers and told Cleveland fans that a new era was about to begin. "We can't promise miracles overnight," he said, "but we can promise that we are going to build a winner in Cleveland." True to his prediction, no sudden miracles occurred, and the team lost another 54 games the following season.

The next campaign also got off to a dismal start, with 19 losses in the first 21 games, before a late surge led by Free landed the Cavaliers in the playoffs for the first time in 7 seasons. The postseason excitement was short-lived, however, as Cleveland was quickly dismissed by a talented Boston lineup.

Although the Cavs would miss the playoffs the next two years, Gund's promise of a winner would soon be realized.

COURTSIDE STORIES

THE TED STEPIEN EXPERIENCE

Ted Stepien was almost certainly the worst owner the Cavaliers ever had. Stepien bought the team in 1980 and was in a hurry to make changes. In three years, Cleveland went through six head coaches. Stepien began trading away so many future draft picks that the NBA made a rule limiting how many draft selections could be dealt away. The owner also wanted to make other modifications to the franchise. To widen the club's fan base, he wanted to rename the team the "Ohio Cavaliers" and play some "home" games in New York and Pennsylvania. He even introduced a polka-based team song to be played at the games. The ongoing circus was reflected in the Cavaliers' performance, as they posted records of 28–54, 15–67, and 23–59. In the midst of their worst season, forward Kenny Carr remarked, "Two years of disarray makes it tough, tough to get up for games." Fan interest had plummeted by 1983, causing Stepien to threaten relocating the team to Toronto. Then Gordon Gund bought the franchise, keeping the Cavs in Cleveland and ending an ugly chapter in NBA history.

NEW RECRUITS
TAKE CHARGE

HOT ROD WILLIAMS BECAME KNOWN FOR UNSELFISH OFFENSE AND POWERHOUSE DEFENSE.

Beginning in 1986, the Cavaliers organization experienced a major overhaul. Gund hired Wayne Embry as general manager and former Cavs guard Lenny Wilkens as head coach. With this new leadership in place, the franchise revamped the player roster with the best single draft in team history. With the team's top two picks in the 1986 NBA Draft, Cleveland selected seven-foot center Brad Daugherty and explosive guard Ron Harper. In a deal with the Dallas Mavericks, Cleveland also acquired the draft rights to sharpshooting point guard Mark Price. Joining this rookie trio was 6-foot-11 forward/center John "Hot Rod" Williams, who had been drafted the previous season but had not yet seen playing time.

The 1986–87 Cavaliers improved upon the previous year's record by just two wins, going 31–51, but there was reason for optimism. Harper, Daugherty, and Williams

JORDAN SINKS THE CAVS

Clevelanders have endured many bitter sports losses throughout the years, but the most bitter may have occurred on May 7, 1989. In 1988–89, the Cavaliers had enjoyed their best regular season in team history, and postseason expectations were high. In the first round of the playoffs, the Cavaliers traded blows with the Chicago Bulls, leading to a deciding Game 5 confrontation. With just three seconds remaining in that contest, Cavs guard Craig Ehlo made a layup, giving Cleveland a 100–99 lead. But following a timeout, Chicago's star guard, Michael Jordan, burst free to get the ball. He then cut back toward the lane, stopped on a dime, and elevated high to hit a double-clutch, 16-foot jump shot over Ehlo's outstretched fingertips. The Cavs and their fans were crushed. "After I made that layup, the building was so deafening, you couldn't hear yourself think," Ehlo said. "And then, Michael makes the shot, and you could hear a pin drop. My reaction was our fans' reaction. For a long time, people in Cleveland thought that there was a curse on us."

emerged as the team's top three scorers, and each was named to the NBA's All-Rookie team. These youngsters continued to shine the following season, and fellow second-year player Price emerged as a standout at the point position. His net-scorching shooting accuracy perfectly complemented Daugherty's rock-steady post play, Harper's highflying athleticism, and Williams's toughness and hustle. All the team lacked now was experience.

Coach Wilkens and the Cavs addressed that concern by trading for talented veteran forwards Larry Nance and Mike Sanders late in 1987–88. Nance, a long-limbed power forward, was as efficient as he was exciting, and he helped the Cavaliers finish 42–40—their first winning mark in 10 seasons. Cleveland put up a fight against the Chicago Bulls in the first round of the playoffs but was beaten in the deciding contest of the five-game series.

In 1988–89, Daugherty, Price, Nance, Harper, and Williams all averaged more than 10 points a game, and Cleveland enjoyed its best season yet, going 57–25. In the playoffs, the Cavs once again faced the Bulls and their superstar, guard Michael Jordan. In another five-game series,

A SOARING VERTICAL EARNED THE OFT-AIRBORNE WORLD B. FREE THE NICKNAME "PRINCE OF MIDAIR."

INTRODUCING...

MARK PRICE

POSITION GUARD
HEIGHT 6 FEET
CAVALIERS SEASONS
1986–95

Physically, Mark Price did not stand out in a crowd. He was average in height, average in build, and sported a haircut that might be seen on a banker. However, when it came to shooting a basketball, he was anything but average. Price had a quick release and perfect form. Whether taking midrange jumpers, arcing shots from the foul line, or hoisting long bombs from three-point range, Price was among the premier marksmen in the history of the NBA. In 1992–93 and 1993–94, Price showcased his uncanny accuracy by winning the NBA's annual Long Distance Shootout competition during the All-Star Game weekend. While Price's claim to fame was his on-target shooting, he was more than willing to share scoring chances with his teammates and was consistently among the league leaders in assists. Price had a knack for navigating around defenders near the basket, and then dishing to teammates for easy buckets. Still, even among those teammates, he'll always be remembered for his marksmanship. As Cavs center Brad Daugherty once said, "He's probably the greatest shooter in NBA history."

> ## "IT'S BEEN A GREAT SEVEN YEARS WITH THE CAVALIERS. HOWEVER, I THINK IT'S TIME TO MOVE ON."
> — LENNY WILKENS ON HIS RESIGNATION

the teams fought to a two-games-to-two tie. Playing at home, Cleveland held a 100–99 lead in the final seconds of Game 5 before Jordan hit a dramatic, game-winning jumper. The loss was a terrible blow, but the youthful Cavaliers were certain there would be more chances. "Our best days are ahead of us," Price said.

Unfortunately, before the Cavaliers would see good days again, they would suffer setbacks. Early in the 1989–90 season, Cleveland dealt away Harper and three future draft picks in a trade that worked out poorly for the Cavs. Health issues also hindered Cleveland's prospects, as Daugherty, Nance, Price, and Williams all suffered injuries over the course of the next 2 seasons, missing a combined 183 games. With its stars sidelined, Cleveland's win totals dropped both years.

The Cavaliers charged back in 1991–92, putting together another 57–25 season. In the postseason, Cleveland topped the New Jersey Nets in four games and then the Boston Celtics in seven to reach the Eastern Conference finals. There, it once again faced the Bulls. The two old foes battled fiercely for six games before the Bulls triumphed. The next year, Cleveland had another strong season, only to exit the playoffs at the hands of the tormenting Bulls once again.

Following that defeat, Lenny Wilkens resigned as head coach, saying, "It's been a great seven years with the Cavaliers. However, I think it's time to move on."

Cleveland hoped that new coach Mike Fratello could guide the Cavs to the next level. Unfortunately, the injury bug plagued the Cavaliers, and what remained of the promising team built in the late 1980s soon dissolved. Following the 1993–94 season, back problems forced Daugherty—a five-time All-Star—to end his playing career after just eight NBA seasons. Nance called it quits, too, and Price would remain just one more season. An era had ended in Cleveland.

THE ONE THAT GOT AWAY

Beginning with a remarkable 1986 NBA Draft and continuing with some excellent trades the following seasons, Cleveland seemed to make all the right roster moves in the late '80s. In three short years, the Cavaliers went from a league doormat to an NBA powerhouse. Cleveland's insightful front office suffered one noteworthy hiccup in 1989, however. Early in the 1989–90 season, the Cavaliers traded talented guard Ron Harper, plus three future draft picks, to the Los Angeles Clippers for forwards Reggie Williams and Danny Ferry. Williams would play only 32 unimpressive games in Cleveland. The 6-foot-10 Ferry would remain with the team 10 years but was underwhelming, averaging 7.8 points and just 3 rebounds per game despite his size. Meanwhile, Harper averaged 19.3 points per game during his 5 years with the Clippers before moving on to help the Chicago Bulls and Los Angeles Lakers win 5 combined NBA titles. The trade is still controversial and its reasoning unclear. One Cleveland reporter noted, "Even 20 years later, the emotions involving the Ferry–Ron Harper trade are very raw."

29

BACK TO SQUARE ONE

SPORTS ILLUSTRATED CALLED TERRELL BRANDON "THE BEST PLAYER YOU'VE NEVER HEARD OF."

leveland entered the mid-1990s in rebuilding mode. The Cavs had a new coach, new players, and a new stadium called Gund Arena. The new roster was composed of an unspectacular but hardworking crew. Players such as forwards Tyrone Hill and Danny Ferry and guards Terrell Brandon and Bobby Phills did not have the offensive firepower of their predecessors, but they aimed to compensate for it by embracing Fratello's philosophy regarding defense.

Cleveland's strategy involved slowing down the game. The new-look Cavs walked the ball up the court and patiently passed it around, waiting for a good shot to present itself. On defense, the team played a tight, swarming style. Cleveland's approach may not have been glamorous, but it was effective. The Cavaliers posted

31

CAVS FASHION

Fashion is always changing, and fashion in the NBA is no exception. But the Cavaliers seem to have taken trendiness to another level. Since 1970, the Cavaliers have changed their uniforms 10 times. The longest they've ever kept one style was seven years, and three of their designs lasted just two years. The first Cleveland uniforms were wine- (brownish-red) and gold-colored and classically designed, but in 1983, the team's colors changed to burnt orange, white, and royal blue. The 1983 uniforms were also the first to have "Cavs" printed on them instead of "Cavaliers" or "Cleveland." The styles and color shades kept changing until 2003, when the Cavaliers went back to their roots—wine and gold—and implemented an updated logo design. The Cavs' roster was also "redesigned" that year to include Ohio native LeBron James, and James's number 23 Cavaliers jersey quickly rocketed to the top of the NBA's best-selling apparel list. Cleveland's duds changed yet again in 2010, reverting to simple trim and block lettering. Old-time Cavs Austin Carr and Campy Russell helped unveil the retro-styled uniforms. But they couldn't help but notice that even if the graphics were old-school, the cut of the shorts was not. Said Carr, "We wore Daisy Dukes."

AS A ROOKIE, QUICK-HANDED BREVIN KNIGHT LED THE NBA IN TOTAL STEALS (196).

winning records each season from 1994–95 to 1997–98 and emerged as the league's stingiest defensive team, allowing fewer than 90 points per game on average. "I'd rather win ugly than lose pretty," Coach Fratello said. Cleveland earned playoff berths in its first three seasons under Fratello but was eliminated in the first round each time.

Although Cleveland's defensive experiment kept the club competitive, the team lacked the scoring punch it needed to really compete in the playoffs. In 1997, the Cavaliers took a new approach, revamping their roster in an effort to improve their offense. Brandon and Phills moved on, and the team added two talented rookies—speedy point guard Brevin Knight and 7-foot-3 Lithuanian center Zydrunas Ilgauskas. Cleveland also traded for

INTRODUCING...

LARRY NANCE

POSITION FORWARD
HEIGHT 6-FOOT-10
CAVALIERS SEASONS
1988–94

Larry Nance first entered the NBA spotlight by winning the league's inaugural Slam Dunk Contest in 1984, earning him the nickname "The High-Ayatollah of Slamola." Also known simply as "Leapin' Larry," Nance's combination of size and jumping ability allowed him to reach heights few opponents could match. During some of his especially highflying jams, Nance actually had to tilt his head to the side so that it wouldn't hit the rim. Yet for all the excitement his dunks could add to a game, Nance's greatest contributions to his teams were versatility and consistency. In 11 of his 13 NBA seasons, Nance averaged more than 16 points and 8 rebounds per game. Nance didn't take a huge number of shots, but he usually cashed in on his attempts. Still, defense may have been his strongest suit. During his career, Nance blocked more shots (2,027) than any other forward in NBA history, and he was named to the league's All-Defensive team three times. "You knew that you couldn't lay the ball up soft," said Cavs forward John Williams. "[If] you did, it was going back the other way."

"I GOT A LOT OF LOVE FOR THESE GUYS, BUT IT GOT TO THE POINT WHERE I DIDN'T EVEN WANT TO PLAY ANYMORE."

— DARIUS MILES ON THE MISERABLE 2002-03 SEASON

All-Star forward Shawn Kemp, formerly with the Seattle SuperSonics, and smooth-shooting guard Wesley Person. In 1997–98, the Cavaliers finished a respectable 47–35 but were again quickly eliminated in the playoffs, this time by the Indiana Pacers.

Despite some early signs of success, the rebuilt Cavaliers deteriorated over the next several years. Ilgauskas seemed injury prone and was sidelined for many games as the team began to skid. Three coaching changes and a slew of trades for players such as guard Ricky Davis and forwards Lamond Murray and Darius Miles did little to stop the bleeding. The new acquisitions added talent but not continuity. The Cavs of the early 2000s often appeared to be playing street ball, sporting flashy style, but lacking in teamwork and sound fundamentals. Cleveland lost more and more games, bottoming out at an embarrassing 17–65 mark in 2002–03. Gund Arena was half empty for home games, and, at times, even the players didn't want to be there. After one late-season defeat, Miles admitted, "I got a lot of love for these guys, but it got to the point where I didn't even want to play anymore."

ven as the Cavaliers sank in the standings, the Cleveland area was still abuzz with basketball intrigue. The source of the excitement was high school star LeBron James, who played in nearby Akron, Ohio. The young phenom was already being dubbed "the next Michael Jordan" and had the nickname "King James." Just 18, the brawny forward was billed as the best NBA prospect in the world, and local fans hoped that the Cavs' poor play would translate into the top overall selection in the 2003 Draft. The fans got their wish. Cleveland was awarded the top selection and kept James in Ohio.

ZYDRUNAS ILGAUSKAS EARNED A PLACE AMONG THE CAVS' ALL-TIME LEADING SCORERS.

THE KING'S SHORT REIGN

LeBRON JAMES INCLUDED FANS IN HIS POWDER-THROWING PREGAME RITUAL.

38

The local boy lived up to the hype, leading the team in scoring, earning NBA Rookie of the Year honors, and drawing the national spotlight to Cleveland with his highlight-reel dunks and passes. Ilgauskas shook the injury bug and was an imposing force under the basket on both ends of the court. Behind James and Ilgauskas, Cleveland missed the playoffs by just a single game.

In the off-season of 2004, Cleveland bolstered its lineup by signing high-energy power forward Drew Gooden and drafted Brazilian forward/center Anderson Varejao. The Cavs' strong frontcourt led to a solid 30–20 start, but the club fizzled down the stretch, narrowly missing the postseason again. "I take full credit," said a disappointed James, who had averaged 27.2 points, 7.4 rebounds, and 7.2 assists per game that season. "I am the leader of this team."

Change loomed on the horizon when Quicken Loans founder Dan Gilbert bought the franchise in March 2005. Gund Arena was renamed Quicken Loans Arena, Mike Brown became the club's new head coach, and former Cavalier forward Danny Ferry took over general managerial duties. With new brass calling the shots, Cleveland brought in Larry Hughes, a multitalented guard who was among the league's best pickpockets. Gilbert expressed confidence. "We believe it will be a golden era of basketball for the fans and community of this hardworking and well-deserving town," he said.

Gilbert's "golden era" began with a solid 50-win season in 2005–06. The club also won its first playoff series in 13 years, topping the Washington Wizards with late-game heroics reminiscent of the organization's first-ever playoff series, as Cleveland tallied 3 wins with clutch shots in the closing seconds of games. The Cavs played tough against the Detroit Pistons in the second round but ultimately lost in seven games.

The Cavaliers matched their 50 wins the next season, and were determined to push deeper into the playoffs. This time, they swept past the Wizards easily and overcame the Nets before running into the Pistons again, this time in the Eastern Conference finals. After losing the first two games of the series, Cleveland won four straight, including a phenomenal double-overtime Game 5 in which James scored the team's final 25 points with an array of dunks, fadeaway jumpers, three-pointers, and finger

LeBRON JAMES

POSITION FORWARD
HEIGHT 6-FOOT-8
CAVALIERS SEASONS
2003-10,
2014-PRESENT

When LeBron James was in high school, his basketball games were televised nationally. Fans simply couldn't wait to see "King James," who had the strapping physique of a football player, handled the ball like a point guard, and tested the strength of rims with his explosive dunks. Forgoing college, he became the first overall pick of the 2003 NBA Draft at age 18. Big, athletic, and skilled enough to play many positions well, James was often called a "point forward" and frequently directed the Cavaliers' offense with the ball in his hands. Although a prolific scorer, James was an unselfish team player and often led the Cavs in assists. Yet while crowds appreciated his needle-threading passes, it was James's slams that made him a fan favorite. With his quick feet and slick ball-handling, James often blew past the first opponent, and then he out-jumped and overpowered any remaining defenders on his way to rim-shaking dunks. After Miami Heat guard Damon Jones received one of James's in-your-face jams, reporters asked if he'd been dunked on like that before. Jones admitted, "Yeah, he dunked on me last year, same way." In 2010, James left Cleveland, opting to sign with the Heat, but returned home four years later.

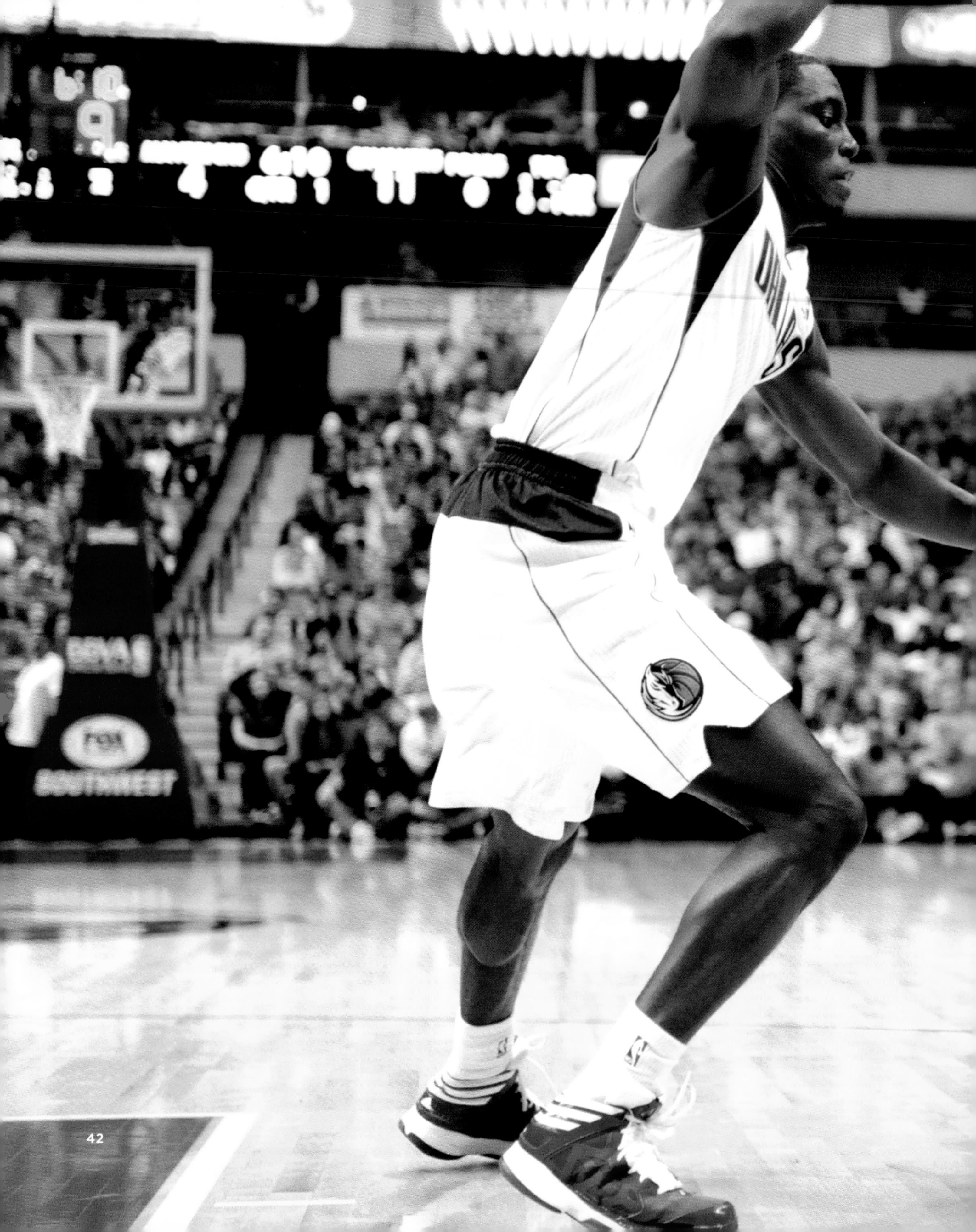
SOUTHWEST

43

A BITTER SPLIT

Many NBA players choose to leave one team and sign with another as a free agent. This can create hard feelings amongst former fans, but perhaps never to the extent as when LeBron James left Cleveland in 2010. Just 25 years old at the time, James was among the league's premier players and the biggest star the Cavaliers had ever had. Talent aside, James had grown up just a short drive from Cleveland and had a "one of us" connection with the locals. So when James announced on a live national broadcast that he would joining the Miami Heat, fans were steamed. Aside from losing a remarkable player, many locals felt their native son was turning his back on blue-collar Cleveland in favor of the gloss and glamour of Miami. This sentiment was compounded when, as part of a publicity event, James strutted and posed like a model with new All-Star teammates Dwyane Wade and Chris Bosh. Adding to the controversy were allegations that this trio had been discussing joining up while they were still on different teams, an act forbidden by the NBA.

rolls. "It was almost just business as usual," Cleveland guard Daniel Gibson said of James's performance. "It just seemed like he was in one of those grooves."

For the first time in their history, the Cavaliers had reached the NBA Finals. There they faced the veteran San Antonio Spurs, a team that had won three NBA titles in the past eight seasons behind star forward Tim Duncan. The Cavs were overwhelmed the first two games in San Antonio. The Spurs then narrowly edged them out the next two games in Cleveland, completing a series sweep.

The 2007–08 Cavs regressed to 45–37, but in 2008–09, the Cavs surged back, as quick new point guard Mo Williams helped Cleveland notch 66 victories. Longtime Cavs announcer Joe Tait noted, "This team has the potential to be the best team ever to wear a Cavs uniform. They're certainly aimed in the right direction."

Unfortunately, the Cavaliers missed their mark, losing to the Orlando Magic in the 2009 Eastern Conference finals. The Cavaliers then tallied an impressive 61–21 record in 2009–10 but were upset by the Celtics in the second round of playoffs.

The disappointment of that postseason defeat was nothing compared with what came two months later. When James announced that he was leaving Cleveland to join the Miami Heat, Cavaliers fans were crushed. Gilbert shared those feelings, but he tried to rally Cleveland fans together. "Clearly, this is bitterly disappointing to all of us," the owner wrote in a letter. "The good news is that the ownership team and the rest of the hardworking, loyal, and driven staff over here at your hometown Cavaliers have not betrayed you and never will betray you."

Cleveland needed to rebuild after the loss of James, and new head coach Byron Scott was faced with the task of getting the remaining players to work as a balanced unit without their star. This was no easy task, and that season, Cleveland finished 19–63. That lousy record earned Cleveland the first pick in the 2011 Draft, which it used on shifty Duke University point guard Kyrie Irving. Irving provided much-needed guidance on the floor and averaged 18.5 points per game. Even so, the Cavaliers again finished last in the Central Division.

The following off-season, Cleveland drafted guard Dion Waiters, who'd proven to be a dangerous scorer in the college ranks. Health issues ended Varejao's 2012–13 season early on, but second-year forward Tristan Thompson stepped up to provide rebounding and interior scoring. With such promising youth and depth, Cleveland appeared primed for its next surge. In 2013–14, that surge was led by Waiters and Irving, and Irving especially stood out as the MVP of the 2014 All-Star Game. But in July, the spotlight shifted to Cleveland's prodigal son, James, who decided to return home to Ohio for 2014–15. Season tickets sold out within 10 hours.

Although the Cavaliers have had their share of bogged down, soggy, and stormy moments, they—like their home city—have also proven that hard work and resourcefulness can overcome challenges. And like a true cavalry, the Cavaliers' greatest successes have resulted from daring leadership, tight teamwork, and individual heroics. With that in mind, Clevelanders eagerly await the Cavaliers' charge that will earn them the ultimate victory—their first NBA title.

INDEX